. UTH

ALSO BY DAVE HASLAM

Manchester, England: The Story of the Pop Cult City

Adventures on the Wheels of Steel: The Rise of the Superstar DJs

Not Abba: The Real Story of the 1970s

Life After Dark: A History of British Nightclubs & Music Venues

Sonic Youth Slept On My Floor: Music, Manchester, and More

WE THE YOUTH

Keith Haring's New York Nightlife

DAVE HASLAM

First published in the UK by Cōnfingō Publishing, 2019

249 Burton Road, Didsbury, Manchester, M20 2WA
www.confingopublishing.uk

Design & Typesetting by Zoë McLean, zoe@confingopublishing.uk

Printed and bound by TJ International Ltd

A CIP catalogue record for this book is available from the British Library

ISBN 978-0-9955966-4-1

2 4 6 8 10 9 7 5 3 1

To the boys and girls at
Drunk At Vogue, with love.

The first half of 1982 was an averagely busy few months in the always hectic life of Keith Haring. He was living in an apartment at 325 Broome Street in the Lower East Side of Manhattan. The tenancy was Samantha McEwen's. To get from her bedroom to the bathroom, she had to walk through Keith's bedroom, a space he shared with his lover, Juan Dubose. For privacy's sake, Keith and Juan slept on a mattress in a camping tent they'd erected in their room.

The shared kitchen and their bedroom were full of Keith's own drawings, the paintings and drawings of his friends, and tags drawn by guests at parties in the apartment. The kitchen walls were covered with graffiti, and the refrigerator too. Keith painted one of his most recognisable images – the so-called 'radiant baby' – on the apartment's front door. In his journal he explained that the reason the baby had become his logo or signature was that 'it is the purest and most positive experience of human existence'.[1]

There would be music playing almost constantly in the apartment. Juan was a DJ; he spent hours playing records and making cassette mixtapes of new or favourite tunes. Keith would take Juan's homemade cassettes and a boom box to wherever he was working that day.

Keith had eclectic music taste. He loved the B-52s; he embraced Brazilian and African music, and challenging performers like Klaus Nomi, but also Top 40 acts; the Grateful Dead were an early and abiding passion; he asked the then barely known Afrika Bambaataa to DJ at the opening of one of his Mudd Club exhibitions; and he fell in love with, and to, records he'd hear Larry Levan play at Paradise Garage, like Gwen Guthrie's 'It Should Have Been You'.

Throughout his life, anyone who encountered Keith marvelled at how passionate about his work he was. Barbara Schwartz first encountered him when he was enrolled at the School of Visual Arts (SVA) where she taught. Later she recalled that he was a compulsive worker, full of energy. 'He worked non-stop,' she told John Gruen, Haring's official biographer.

He was the epitome of 'work hard, play hard'. The two things, in fact, often combined. One of the key venues in Keith's nightlife during the years immediately after his arrival in New York in 1978 was Club 57, which was located in the basement of a Polish church on St Mark's Place. At Club 57, you could dress up as a beatnik, dance to the B-52s, and watch experimental art videos on a loop, all on the same night.

Club 57 was a significant example of a handful of clubs and venues in Manhattan at various times between 1978 and 1985 that featured music performances alongside art exhibitions, and film and video shows. Over the next pages we'll celebrate these spaces, their crucial role as catalysts for cultural activity. We'll hear of clubs that became art galleries and an art gallery that turned into a club.

There was a collective energy around such venues in that era. They were cheap places (cheap to run and cheap to attend), which nurtured ad hoc communities and also a sense of potential. They summed up one of Patti Smith's most positive visions, in her song 'Land': a 'sea of possibilities'.

---

1 Keith Haring, *Journals* (Penguin, 2010), 132.

Through most of 1979 and 1980, Keith spent at least one night a week at Club 57. There would often be no more than three dozen people in attendance. He described the venue as 'our hangout, a clubhouse, where we could do whatever we wanted'. Club 57 was the first venue in New York where he exhibited his work (for one night only), characteristically described on the invitations as an 'exhibition and dance party'.

Nothing lasts for ever: not youth, not life, and certainly not nightclubs. Tier 3 was a restaurant in TriBeCa that reinvented itself in May 1979 as a live music venue with a three-hundred capacity. Bartender-turned-live-music-booker Hilary Jaeger booked John Lurie's band the Lounge Lizards, and the likes of Liquid Liquid, and also several British acts, including the Slits, the Pop Group and Young Marble Giants. But Tier 3 lasted barely eighteen months before the owners decided to turn it into a country-western bar.

Danceteria had opened at its first location on 252 West 37th Street, but moved on after a couple of years (it ended up moving six times). Its most successful era was when it was located in 21st Street from 1982 onwards, featuring DJs Mark Kamins, Jody Kurilla, and former Mudd Club DJ Anita Sarko on the decks. And once the venue had hired booker Ruth Polsky, Danceteria hit heights of credibility and success. One of the reasons why Tier 3 closed was that it couldn't compete with Danceteria.

By 1982, Club 57 was on the wane. If Keith wasn't there, then perhaps he'd be at the Mudd Club, where, after the success of Club 57, he'd been invited to curate art exhibitions on the venue's fourth floor; or maybe at Danceteria (he'd worked there as a busboy, clearing tables during the summer of 1980, at its first location); or maybe he'd be out wandering the streets with Fab 5 Freddy.

Keith lived, worked and played in downtown Manhattan, where the streets were post-industrial, ungentrified, druggy, desolate. It was a very different side to New York to the glamour and the stars of Studio 54. The habitués of the uptown clubs and shops would avoid downtown, but to young creatives, the low rents and the empty buildings had an irresistible appeal.

The last vestiges of the East Village rag trade were more or less the only signs of life during the day, and once the garment workers had cleared out of the sweatshops and the small factories had closed in the early evening, the streets were abandoned. New York was said to be financially bankrupt, many of the city's warehouses and workshops were empty, semi-derelict, but these spaces became the playground of a generation of artists, musicians, poets, performers, party people, dropouts, designers, and underground film-makers.

They injected life into downtown Manhattan via experimentation and collaboration. From November 1978 a group of artists called Colab (Collaborative Projects) hosted exhibitions in abandoned buildings. In the spring of 1980, they took over premises that had been a massage parlour. The *Times Square Show*, as it was called, featured art, video, performance, fashion shows, and film screenings.

It turned out to be notable for several reasons. One was the variety and quality of the work by the likes of Keith, Candace Hill-Montgomery, Coleen Fitzgibbon, Kenny Scharf, and Jenny Holzer. In addition, partnering with the Fashion Moda organisation in South Bronx brought quality graffiti art into the *Times Square Show*, including work by Lee Quiñones and Fab 5 Freddy. Keith met these two artists for the first time at the show.

It was a telling moment of synchronicity; downtown artists were creating works in a bankrupt city, and in another dilapidated part of New York – above 125th Street in Harlem and the South Bronx

– graffiti was a burgeoning form of artistic self-expression. 'Graffiti was at a high point then, the early eighties,' Fab 5 Freddy later recalled. 'Every train, every subway car was completely blitzed.'[2]

Artists of all kinds were making something in, or indeed out of, the debris of their city. In a very literal sense: on one occasion, Keith and Angel Ortiz (LAII) decorated a battered yellow taxi hood.

Keith collaborated many times with LAII, but his closest ally from the graffiti world was probably Fab 5 Freddy. Keith told John Gruen that it was Freddy who introduced him to Paradise Garage, the club that would become Keith's second home: 'It was maybe 2:00 A.M. and we were high and in the West Village. We came to King Street, just off Seventh Avenue and there's this place. It's packed, and maybe 70 percent of the kids are black, 20 percent are Spanish, and 10 percent are Oriental and white.'

Paradise Garage was only open Fridays and Saturdays. Saturday was the gay night. Keith became addicted to Saturday nights there. In subsequent years, when trips to Europe were scheduled, he'd still do everything to be in New York on weekends so that

---

[2] From an interview given in 1997, http://www.haring.com/!/selected_writing/conversations# (consulted August 2019).

he could visit Paradise Garage. It was there, in May 1984, around the time of his twenty-sixth birthday, that Keith hosted an event he dubbed 'Party of Life', which included a short performance by an emerging New York talent called Madonna.

Keith loved to throw a party. At the end of 1983, he held a New Year's Eve party and covered the walls of a studio/gallery space with his artwork. He spent at least some of the night DJ'ing. The audience were treated to songs including 'Tour De France' by Kraftwerk, In Deep 'Last Night a DJ Saved My Life', Peech Boys 'On A Journey', World Premiere 'Share The Night', 'Jam On Revenge (The Wikki-Wikki Song)' by Newcleus, and 'Work For Love' by Ministry. A beautiful, eclectic mix.

Keith had first seen Madonna perform at a club called the Funhouse over at 526 West 26th Street where Madonna's boyfriend John 'Jellybean' Benitez was the resident DJ, playing a mix of electro, new wave and hip-hop to a Hispanic and Italian-American audience. Jellybean was involved in the making of Madonna's first album; he remixed three tracks and produced 'Holiday'.

For the 'Party of Life', Keith and LAII decorated the venue and produced invitations printed dayglo and black on handkerchieves. The club filled to capacity, most of the hottest Paradise Garage regulars attended, and Keith wore a yellow velvet dayglo tuxedo made for him by one of his closest friends, Bobby Breslau.

The DJ at Paradise Garage was Larry Levan. Described as 'godlike' by Keith, Levan played at the 'Party of Life', alongside Juan Dubose.[3] In 1986, Keith produced a work honouring Levan; a drawing of the DJ, with his head emanating rays of energy, his hands manipulating dancing figures.

It's possible that some records rocked both dancefloors: Strafe's 'Set It Off', for example, or 'Weekend' by Class Action. But the audiences were different. Larry Levan's Saturdays at Paradise Garage were gay nights, but the Funhouse was a straight club. Jellybean would play Talking Heads records, reggae, new wave, electro boogie, and South Bronx B-boy classics like 'The Mexican' by Babe Ruth.[4] Larry Levan played Blondie and the Clash, but his playlist was dominated by dance music with black gospel roots, lots of underground disco; in New York, disco, and then house, was more popular with the

---

[3] Juan played some decent gigs, including regular appearances at Area, a club at 157 Hudson Street that opened in 1983.

[4] In 1984, Jellybean produced a new version of 'The Mexican' with the original Babe Ruth singer Jenny Haan. It topped the US dance charts.

gay crowd.

Keith's nights out gave him so much; from a sense of life to a direct influence on the way he created his art. Barbara Schwartz, who'd picked up on his energy and dedication at the very beginning of his time at the School of Visual Arts, soon identified something else about his work. It was almost synonymous with music, she said: 'His stuff had syncopation, a kind of beat he must have found in the clubs he was going to.'[5]

+

Keith Haring grew up in Kutztown, Pennsylvania, a community a hundred and twenty miles from New York City, but metaphorically much further. His parents were conservative in attitudes and politics: they voted for Nixon, supported the Vietnam War, and forbade Keith from buying bell-bottoms when he was eleven. In amongst tensions with his parents, there was one activity that bonded Keith with his father: drawing. His father, Allen, liked to draw cartoons, and encouraged Keith to do the same.

Around the time he craved bell-bottoms, one of his favourite activities was following the adventures of the Monkees in their TV sitcom series. He cut out photographs of the Monkees from teen magazines, and developed a particular interest in Davy Jones (he later described Davy as 'the cute, young one'). He started a Monkees fan club.

He discovered the Grateful Dead and then angel dust, which duly became his latest obsession. Keith never seemed to lose this; once he'd discovered something that turned him on, he'd devote himself to it ultra-enthusiastically. 'I remember that all the anti-drug things on television at the time only made me want to do them more,' he told David Sheff in an interview published in *Rolling Stone* magazine in 1989.[6] 'They showed all these things to scare you: a gas burner turning into a beautiful flower. I thought, that's great! You mean I can see like *that*?'

Later, when he'd worked out less destructive ways to use drugs, he described angel dust as 'a stupid drug', and admitted that in this period he'd been a mess, and 'an embarrassment to the family'.[7] His mother confessed to John Gruen that 'it was also a relief not to have the loud music going all the time' when Keith left home and moved to Pittsburgh in

---

[5] John Gruen, *Keith Haring: The Authorized Biography* (Fireside, 1991), 38.
[6] David Sheff, 'Keith Haring, An Intimate Conversation', *Rolling Stone*, 10 August 1989.
[7] Ibid.

September 1976.[8]

He went to Pittsburgh with the intention of training to become a commercial artist and graphic designer but didn't stick with the course. That's not to say he wasn't deeply interested in art, and the study and theory of it. He was never a naïve artist; he knew the historical and cultural context.

Paul Klee once remarked: 'A line is a dot that went for a walk.' Keith took a deep interest in artists like Paul Klee, Mark Tobey, and Jean Dubuffet, their art and their words. He took as gospel Dubuffet's belief that art could and should happen in all kinds of places and reach all kinds of people. As early as 1978, while at college, Keith produced an artistic manifesto which included the statement: 'Art is for everybody.'

From late 1977 into 1978, Keith had a maintenance job at the Pittsburgh Arts and Crafts Center, which entailed everything from painting walls to helping fix the roof. Amongst his memories of those times was the impact his work colleagues had on him. They were mostly from black inner city Pittsburgh, with backgrounds very different to his: 'I was working very intimately with maybe five or six of these black guys, and I felt very sexually drawn to some of them. With others, it was a camaraderie sort of thing.

But what was also important, was that I was being exposed to a whole other culture, which was completely different from the sixties, the leftover hippie thing that I was still living out.'[9]

His black colleagues were listening to funkier music than he was, turning him on to the likes of 'Flash Light' by Parliament. Keith was also becoming aware of punk and new wave, including the scene around CBGB in New York. He was reassessing his music tastes, and cut his hair, and developed an interest in what he called the 'artsy side' of new wave music (his favourite album of 1978 was the Devo debut, *Q: Are We Not Men? A: We Are Devo!*).

Although his job was in the maintenance department, Keith acted like he was a student at the Center, attending printmaking classes, and making lithographs and etchings. He even took an opportunity to mount an exhibition of his work, eventually coming to the conclusion he needed to be in New York: 'I decided to make a major break. New York was the only place to go.'[10]

He lived for a while on West Tenth Street but decided to share a place with one of his old Kutztown

---

[8] Gruen, 24.
[9] Ibid., 28.
[10] Ibid., 32.

friends, Drew Straub, in the East Village, on First Avenue between First and Second Street. The apartment was in a building directly across from the Club Baths, one of many established bath houses where gay men would meet for anonymous (usually) sexual encounters.

A few months earlier, while still in Pittsburgh, Keith had had his first sexual experience with a man, and had discovered the attractions of cruising, especially in a park close to his apartment. His work and his world were opening up: 'I was happy, because I suddenly found that my art was blossoming, as was my sexuality, and opportunities seemed at hand.'

Arriving in New York to study at the School of Visual Arts in 1978, living alongside the gay bars and bath houses, he later recalled: 'The whole gay thing was everywhere. I mean, it was almost too much. You couldn't go to the post office without cruising or being cruised – without being totally aware of sex.'

The more he went to the baths, the more he preferred the atmosphere there to the cruising scenes in the bars. 'Everyone was just wearing a towel, so you weren't judged by what you were wearing... all class distinctions were gone,' he later explained. 'You were a common, united, connected group of people.'[11]

He remained a visitor to the baths even after he'd settled into a domestic life with Juan. We all have our favoured spaces, our trails through our home towns or cities, and our routines. You feel out of place, you go looking for a place.

Even after a big night out, he wouldn't sleep all day. At the Broome Street apartment he'd wake, carefully pick out a T-shirt, put on those glasses any style-spotter would be forgiven for describing as 'nerdy'; all set to spend the day making things happen, for himself, and for his allies. Not forgetting to grab the boom box and press play.

+

By the early months of 1982, Keith Haring had gained much notoriety for one particular activity: chalk drawing in subway stations. One day, riding the subway, he saw an empty black panel where an advertisement was supposed to go. He went to a card shop and bought a box of white chalk; he started drawing in the black spaces. These chalk drawings didn't require studio space, or much of a financial outlay, or the patronage of the art establishment, but were guaranteed an audience.

---

[11] Ibid., 30-43.

A distinctive vocabulary of images he'd developed during preparations for an exhibition at Club 57 began to feature on the subway panels, including crawling babies, dogs, and flying saucers. The subways could be places of tension and violence; the drawings were a fragile and joyful intervention into that world.

His profile rising through 1982 – with a show in Rotterdam's Galerie 't Venster and prospective art buyers incessantly knocking on his studio door – Keith decided to make some accommodation with the gallery scene, and agreed to do a one-man show in October of that year, in a New York gallery in SoHo owned by Tony Shafrazi.

He was already using his art – and, when necessary, his notoriety – to give support to progressive causes. In 1982, he fashioned a poster for an anti-nuke rally in Central Park, printed and handed out twenty thousand copies. The poster featured the radiant baby trapped in a mushroom cloud; overwhelming violence threatening purity and the future.

A few years earlier he'd made other disruptive public art interventions, mocking up newspaper headlines, including RONALD REAGAN ACCUSED OF TV STAR SEX DEATH; KILLED AND ATE LOVER and REAGAN'S DEATH COPS

HUNT POPE, and pasting them on walls.

A few other artists were pursuing similar methods to connect with audiences – including Jenny Holzer, who'd printed slogans and cryptic phrases on posters. In addition, Jean-Michel Basquiat's first work was in many ways a type of literary graffiti, or 'punk/haiku poetry', as it was called by art critic Jeffrey Deitch.[12]

Like Keith, Basquiat's passion for music was strong, as was his desire to participate and create. Basquiat fronted an experimental art noise quartet called Gray; produced the single 'Beat Bop'; and would occasionally DJ at venues like Tier 3. His involvement at Tier 3 also included painting a mural on the wall between the bar and the music room. He did it for expenses only (the cost of the spray paint).[13]

In 1982, Basquiat had a brief affair with Madonna. When his long-time girlfriend, Suzanne Mallouk, found out about the relationship, she confronted Madonna at the Roxy. Basquiat later depicted the ensuing brawl in a piece of art called *A Panel of Experts*, referring to Suzanne as Venus and naming

---

[12] Jeffrey Deitch in Jeffrey Deitch, Suzanne Geiss, Julia Gruen, *Keith Haring* (Rizzoli, 2008), 17.

[13] Basquiat made a cameo as a DJ in Blondie's video for 'Rapture', although it is believed he secured the role only because Grandmaster Flash didn't show up.

Madonna.

In October 1981, Juan Dubose became the subject for a Keith Haring drawing within just weeks of their first encounter, which had taken place at St Mark's Baths. An extravagant celebration of Juan's ejaculation, the work was entitled *Jerk Off (Juan Dubose)*.[14]

In common with many of the artists (and musicians and film-makers) of the downtown scene, neither Haring nor Basquiat appeared to see limits to what artistic media were available to them, and the art of both reflected the mess or joy of their love life, for example, and their passions and inspirations, including music.

Grace Jones writes about Keith in her book *I'll Never Write My Memoirs* (she was introduced to him by Andy Warhol). She remembers Keith at the Paradise Garage watching the dancers, their 'hands up in the air, banging up against each other, life bursting around them'.[15]

On one occasion, Keith and Kenny Scharf went to see Fab 5 Freddy and Futura 2000, who were throwing a party at their studio, attended by members of the Rock Steady Crew. When the breakdancers took to the floor, Keith was fascinated, especially by the dancers spinning on their heads.

Keith approached a drawing almost in the same spirit as dancers on a dancefloor. Other artists make a sketch, or start with a grid, but not Keith. Keith would skip the planning stage, start in the upper-left corner of the wall, or paper, or tarpaulin, and draw in perfect rhythm, rarely stopping for breath or missing a beat.

It was as if he was taking all his influences, walking a few blocks with them, spinning them round like a record, and then starting to draw his strong lines directly, fluidly. Not so much a dot that went for a walk, as a dot that went for a dance.

+

By the end of 1980, Keith had moved on from sharing with Drew Straub and was living in an apartment with Kenny Scharf near Times Square. He'd met Kenny at SVA and they'd become good friends. Kenny's art was colourful, dayglo, super-realistic; he also liked to spray-paint and customise household appliances, TVs, kettles.

Samantha McEwen was another SVA student; she'd first met Keith in 1978. In 1980, she was

---

[14] The drawing recently sold for $100,000.
[15] Grace Jones, *I'll Never Write My Memoirs* (Simon & Schuster, 2015), 205.

dating Kenny. She'd got a place of her own in Broome Street, but spent lots of time at Kenny's. They were close, happy together. Kenny later described the three of them in bed together, watching TV.

After Samantha and Kenny broke up, she moved back to Broome Street and when the landlord gave her an opportunity to take a little more room in the building, she did – and Keith moved in, with Juan. And the two guys built their tent.

I met up with Samantha in London recently. She told me about her years as Keith Haring's friend and housemate, from nights out, and evenings in, to being enlisted to hand out anti-nuke posters in Central Park. She also said that there was a tarpaulin factory opposite the Broome Street apartment, which prompted Keith to begin painting on them: vinyl paint on vinyl tarp.

She also pointed out how important to the Keith Haring story Juan Dubose was: 'Juan has not been properly written into history, he was so fantastic. He was the most beautiful, quietest, most devoted, most monosyllabic guy. He'd cook delicious meals for Keith – it was their little love nest.'

Samantha is English, but her mother was American, from Manhattan. Her older sister went over to fashion school in New York. Samantha followed her, to attend Sarah Lawrence College, a liberal arts college forty minutes from Manhattan. But the lure of the city was too much; she switched her studies to SVA. In her first weeks there she made friends with Keith and Bruno Schmidt and others, and met John Sex in printmaking class.

The Mudd Club opened and she started going there, with that group of friends from SVA: 'You'd walk from the Lower East Side through SoHo, through Broadway, it was completely empty, there wasn't a light on after five o'clock. It was so wild and so beautiful, you'd walk these empty streets, and then you'd get to White Street, and you'd be at the Mudd Club.'

The Mudd Club's founders were publicist Steve Mass, singer Anya Phillips, and art curator Diego Cortez (who also had great connections in some of the most avant-garde parts of the New York music scene). Despite (or because of) Studio 54 grabbing headlines with its stars and glamour, the three knew there was demand for a counterpoint to sleek uptown chic, a black-walled anti-disco for arty weirdos.

The Mudd hosted new wave and no wave bands, and the DJs played punk, new wave, and rockabilly. The B-52s featured on the club's opening night, Hallowe'en 1978. Keith went to see the B-52s as often as he could, often with Kenny, or Drew, or John Sex: 'We would stand at the front and idol-worship,' said Keith.

It's not hard to imagine him singing along to the list of real and imagined marine animals in 'Rock Lobster' – after all, he shared a love for colour and joy, and forms of expression that oscillated between the figurative and the abstract. Plus there was the appeal of the band's camp, joyful stage show.

Drew Straub later shared one of his most vivid memories of his time as Keith's roommate: 'Keith would be sitting in our kitchen and he'd put on "Rock Lobster" – and he'd sit there and draw and he'd leave the record on for, like, eight or ten hours.' He also remembers what he liked to draw: 'Penises in a kind of all-over pattern.'[16]

One of Samantha's abiding memories of living with Keith was how he was equal to any situation. 'He met someone, he would engage them. He was super curious. He would always talk to me about his interests and what he was reading. He was very interested in the world; living with him was a real education.'

Club 57 sounds like a club full of similarly curious and adventurous people, a tight group of friends.

'Yes, Club 57 was something that very much came out of that group of people. The Mudd Club was run by Steve Mass, it was his thing. Club 57 was a group of friends making things up as they went along. If anyone was in charge, it was Ann Magnuson.'

And it was a small place, wasn't it?

'It was very small, it wasn't commercial or even visible. Keith invited me to Club 57 and gave me a flyer. It was private in some ways – you would only invite friends.'

The B-52s played Club 57 in September 1979. In April 1980, there was a night of various kinds of performance called 'Acts of Live Art', featuring the likes of John Sex, and Drew Straub and Kenny Scharf. Keith Haring went on stage with his head through the frame of an old television set. On a couple of other occasions, he would dress in black and read poems: 'I was, in fact, calling myself a "terrorist poet"', he later explained.[17]

Club 57 opened with a jukebox providing the tunes but then some turntables were installed. DJs were Tom Scully, Naomi Regelson, and Dany

[16] Gruen, 48.

[17] Deitch, Geiss, Gruen, 60.

Johnson. Johnson eventually got most of the work. Her 1980 playlist included Bobby Byrd 'Hot Pants', Count 5 'Psychotic Reaction', Manu Dibango 'Soul Makossa', and 'White Mice' by the Mo-Dettes.

Club 57 regulars were music fans, but the other elements were special: the performances, the art, and, most notably, an accent on video. 'Club 57 people were fascinated by video,' says Samantha. 'The art schools were teaching video as a medium – like a "media" medium – whereas they were using video like they were using spray paint.'

One of Keith's video experiments, 'Tribute to Gloria Vanderbilt', has 'Money' by the Flying Lizards as a soundtrack and reveals Keith to have been an energetic and expressive dancer who looked good in lipstick.

Samantha confirms there was a great dynamic between the housemates: 'It was so youthful and upbeat, but serious too; Kenny and Keith were very seriously trying to get recognition.'

But on their own terms?

'Yes, the aesthetic of Club 57 – the video and graffiti, for example – was so different. They weren't interested in what the galleries could offer them, and what the galleries could offer them wasn't that interesting.'

As Club 57 reveals, just three dozen people is all it takes for a venue to have a life of its own, attracting people with creativity on their mind. Once attracted, anything can happen. Imagine a room including David Byrne, Nan Goldin, Jean-Michel Basquiat, Lydia Lunch, and Klaus Nomi. Club 57 was where Jim Jarmusch showed his first films, and where Keith Haring staged his first New York exhibition, on 21 July 1980.

In the run-up to the 'exhibition and dance party', Keith bought a roll of oak-tag paper, cut it up and spread it over the floor and began drawing. Recognisable images started coming: humans, animals, a dog was zapped with energy rays by a flying saucer, then flying saucers were also zapping the humans.

Without any idea of the genesis of this stuff, it seemed to him that something major was occurring, that he'd broken through. 'They were humans and animals in different combinations. I made this person crawling on all fours, which evolved into the quote-unquote baby... Out of these drawings my entire future vocabulary was born.'[18]

In October 1980, Keith hosted an event

---

[18] Gruen, 57.

at Club 57 featuring art found on the street, art by children and other pieces of 'raw art by unknown authors'.[19] Other nights out at Club 57 included a rap night and a colour Xerox art show.

By the end of 1980, Steve Mass was poaching staff from Club 57. He wanted some of the cultural cachet the smaller venue had. This is Kenny Scharf's interpretation of why Mass was replacing Mudd Club staff: 'He started hiring everyone from Club 57 to man the door and be bartenders. If you're on mushrooms and acid you have a lot more energy than if you're on heroin.'[20]

Keith was invited to take over the fourth floor of the Mudd Club in order to present some art shows. He arranged the *Beyond Words* exhibition in April 1981, which he asked Fab 5 Freddy and Futura 2000 to curate. The show included works by Rammellzee, Lee Quiñones, Lady Pink, and Jean-Michel Basquiat.

Like Keith, Jean-Michel would visit clubs he'd heard good things about, whatever the clientele, the age range, the sexualities. The pair would go to museums (together, and/or with Fab 5 Freddy). From early in their relationship, it was as if they knew they would be linked together in history.

Certainly, by 1982, new chapters were

opening for them both. In that year, Keith's journal entries begin to deal with the idea of success, especially following his exhibition at Galerie 't Venster in Rotterdam and his first show at Tony Shafrazi's gallery. In 1984, he was a part of an exhibition at the Musée d'Art Moderne de la Ville de Paris, alongside Jean-Michel Basquiat, Kenny Scharf, and Robert Combas. During this visit, Helmut Newton photographed Keith in a gold lamé tuxedo for *Vanity Fair*.

Ever aware and thoughtful, Keith could sense a shift towards negativity in how he was being perceived by some people. He tried to accept this, while always disappointed by it. 'As soon as you get some acclaim, you have alienated some people that think that they deserved it instead of you,' he told David Sheff of *Rolling Stone*.

In the same interview, he said that by 1984 he'd had to withdraw from the subway project because people were stealing the pieces. 'I'd go down and draw in the subway, and two hours later every piece would be gone. They were turning up for sale.'

+

The commercial success of Keith Haring and Jean-

[19] Description taken from a flyer for the event, exhibited at Tate Liverpool (2019).
[20] Deitch, Geiss, Gruen, 67.

Michel Basquiat took some of the starry-eyed innocence out of the New York world they were a key part of, but other, macroeconomic, changes in the mid-1980s were having an effect too. The half-forgotten streets of Lower Manhattan were attracting the attentions of property speculators: the increasing value of real estate in the area hastened the demise of the ad hoc venues, the clubs, and the creativity of the downtown art scene.

A rise in commercial rents in the East Village drove the Fun Gallery out of business in 1985, and Danceteria closed in 1986 (it's now an office building). It was the same with loft living: artist David Wojnarowicz's rent more than doubled between 1986 and 1988.

In 1984, Madonna announced she was a material girl living in a material world. In 1986, Gwen Guthrie's 'Ain't Nothin' Goin' On But The Rent' filled Larry Levan's dancefloor, its lyrics insisting 'you got to have a J-O-B if you want to be with me'.

Money was talking, a new New York was taking over. Writer Tim Lawrence explains that the downtown scene began to unravel 'when New York assumed the character of a neoliberal city organized around finance, capital, gentrification, real estate inflation, and social regulation'.[21]

The era of living cheaply in Manhattan and finding space to dream was over: the East Village was on the way to becoming a gentrified commercial and residential neighbourhood. The next generations wouldn't have cheap space downtown; they'd build an infrastructure outside Manhattan – in Brooklyn, and elsewhere.

The story of the art, venues, music and cheap living in Lower Manhattan in Keith Haring's era is a textbook example of a process that's familiar in various post-industrial cities since the mid-1970s. Visionary, under-regulated, underground scenes in semi-derelict spaces in abandoned districts have emerged and caught the imagination, only to see the physical and psychological space for their creativity annexed by big business.

Cities with a thriving culture need more than established mainstream cultural activity. The alternative provided by New York's downtown club scene had been mirrored by the small galleries giving space and breaks to young artists – including graffiti artists – and also by the DIY spirit of the local independent music labels like 99 Records. This is how art

[21] Tim Lawrence, *Life and Death on the New York Dance Floor 1980-1983* (Duke University Press, 2016), xiii.

and culture thrive; oppositional and maverick energies creating new works, and new networks.

As well as native New Yorkers, Keith mixed with Jenny Holzer and Patti Astor, who were from Ohio; Arthur Russell was born in Iowa; Klaus Nomi moved to New York from Germany, Bruno Schmidt from Brazil; Kenny Scharf grew up in southern California, Samantha McEwen was British; Ann Magnuson grew up in Charleston, West Virginia. Keith himself had moved from Pittsburgh.

Outsiders or new arrivals, looking for like-minded folk and for action, and for some place they'd feel they belong: where do they meet? They meet at night. In a venue, after dark. These strangers come together, then catch and surf the collective energy. Performers and audiences alike, caught up in everything, excited, wanting cultural revolution.

Often (but not necessarily uniquely), youth brings with it recklessness and resourcefulness. Stability isn't a virtue, but unpredictability is. There's a hunger, a propensity to absorb experience – what I have elsewhere described as being 'porous'.[22] If you have it, you don't want to lose it.

Grace Jones, talking about Keith, says this: 'He always said he was open to everything and spent his life "gathering information," which is something

I identified with. He gathered a lot of information, about himself and others, at the Garage.'[23]

Especially when coupled with a drive to participate, this adventurousness and porousness is a creative, powerful thing. Even better if you have no fear and don't know what mistakes are. Ann Magnuson, looking back on Club 57, said: 'We didn't let anyone tell us "no". We didn't allow poverty to stop us from realising our wildest imaginings.'[24]

Keith Haring's default position when confronted with something inspiring was an urge to contribute. Fab 5 Freddy has recalled how he and Keith were spellbound by Paradise Garage, but, in addition, he remembers Keith's immediate desire to plan some kind of involvement. Keith told Freddy: 'I want to meet the people that own it. I want to do some art for this place.'

Of course, he did get involved at Paradise Garage, in various ways and on various occasions, not just via hosting the 'Party of Life' event in May 1984. In 1985, Keith painted directly on to Grace Jones's naked body for a performance at Paradise

---

[22] Dave Haslam, *Sonic Youth Slept On My Floor* (Little, Brown 2018), 320.

[23] Jones, 206.

[24] https://www.dazeddigital.com/artsandculture/article/12458/1/east-village-preservation-society-club-57 (consulted August 2019).

Garage. This wasn't the first time he'd drawn on her – that was July 1984, at a photo shoot for Warhol's *Interview* magazine (photographer Robert Mapplethorpe).[25] Grace and Keith bonded beautifully; the way they both moved between disco and new wave and back, seemed symptomatic of so much about their attitudes to life. Grace: 'That was how I saw myself. Always in between, on the way somewhere else.'

Keith chose to make his dancing figures of no determinate gender, race, age, or sexual orientation. He seemed to prize experiences that could initiate the erasure of barriers: the anonymity of the bath houses, the communality of the dancefloor (especially the ethnic mix at Paradise Garage). He lived without barriers between leisure and work. From Warhol, he learned that popular culture and high art existed in the same world of ideas. And what was Keith's description of his first exhibition at Club 57? 'Exhibition and dance party.'

At his second show for Tony Sarfrazi, from December 1983 to January 1984, Keith transformed the Sarfrazi gallery, darkening the room, installing lights and a sound system, and recruiting Juan Dubose to DJ. A gallery had become a nightclub.

In 1986, Keith designed record sleeves for

Emanon's 'The Baby Beat Box' and 'Someone Like You' by Sylvester. The Sylvester single (with a Larry Levan remix on the B-side) topped the American dance charts, and hit over 500,000 sales. What better way for Keith Haring to deliver on his 1978 manifesto pledge 'Art is for everybody' than have his work in record stores, living rooms, and vinyl collections, and next to turntables in nightclubs all around the world?

+

The mid-1980s threw various personal challenges at Keith Haring, including how to manage his career, his profile, and his time, while the community around him struggled to deal with the growing materialism and gentrification of Manhattan, and the loss of cheap spaces to live and work in.

But the biggest, most tragic, challenge was the devastation caused by AIDS. It was a catastrophe suffered by him, his community, and humanity. It was 1985, he later recalled, when he became fully aware of 'the true horror of AIDS'. Communities

---

[25] In 1986, Grace Jones wore a huge skirt painted by Haring for the video of her song 'I'm Not Perfect (But I'm Perfect For You)', and he painted her again for a scene in the movie *Vamp*.

started collapsing, joy was in short supply.

When Juan died, Keith kept on pushing on, and never stopped working. But faced with such an event, the young man equal to any situation was momentarily in turmoil: 'Right now I'm not sure I understand anything anymore.'[26]

Keith lost numerous very close friends, including Bobby Breslau, who died in January 1987. Keith considered him a mentor. In his journal, he confessed that Bobby's death pushed him into 'a new situation of aloneness'.[27] Furthermore, he decided there could never be another 'Party of Life', given Bobby's passing.

Juan Dubose died in 1988, the day after Keith had been to visit him ('I can see he is draining away to nothing,' he wrote in his journal[28]). Although Juan was no longer with Keith – they'd not been lovers for a couple of years – the relationship was the longest, closest of Keith's life: under the tent, out at night dressed in matching white tracksuits and sneakers, in domestic bliss.

A few months after Juan's death, Keith was in Madrid on Valentine's Day, and he returned early from a night out and sat in his hotel room writing in his journal and listening to one of Juan's mixtapes. 'I still find it hard to believe that Juan Dubose is really dead,' he wrote. 'The one thing he left forever was his spirit through music. Even in these tapes of other people's music, somehow his presence is there.'[29]

By this time, Keith had been diagnosed with AIDS, although he didn't make the news public until the middle of 1989. He knew the diagnosis was coming – he'd had symptoms which suggested he was ill, and as early as 1985 he was creating work which appeared to foretell that the illness would claim him; that year, in *Untitled (Self-Portrait)*, he imagined himself with a rash of red spots on his face.

After his diagnosis, Keith acknowledged that the lifestyle he had discovered and enjoyed in his first years in New York – the bath houses, the gay bars and clubs – had been like a 'gay Disneyland'.[30] He was aware of the connection between the freedom and pleasure of that world, and the loss of so many friends from AIDS. And he'd known he was at risk. 'I was living as if it was a reality.'[31]

Between his HIV diagnosis in 1988 and his death in February 1990, he was arguably more pro-

---

[26] *Journals*, 316.
[27] Ibid., 150-154.
[28] Gruen, 195.
[29] *Journals*, 316.
[30] Gruen, 35.
[31] https://walkerart.org/magazine/politics-keith-haring-2 (consulted August 2019).

ductive than ever, including designing a label for Absolut Vodka, and a carousel for an amusement park in Hamburg. During the same period, he went to Chicago where he worked with school kids on a mural and painted two walls in a medical centre. He also went to Antwerp for the opening of an exhibition of his work, and to Paris to work with the painter Erik Bulatov. From Paris he travelled to Pisa in Italy to paint a mural.

Samantha recalls the rupturing of the community in the mid-1980s. 'You find your own people. People had come together, all this had happened. It was so beautiful what was being achieved. And then AIDS came along, that was it. That was their life. And thank God it was amazing...'

You mean, while it lasted?

'While it lasted, yes.'

So, from where you were, the people you were with, I guess AIDS started as a rumour?

'It wasn't anything anyone understood. After the first deaths, it got very confusing, nobody knew how it was carried, and if it was only a gay thing. It invaded all our lives. I remember Keith telling me he had swollen glands and we just assumed it was a bad sign.'

It was so virulent.

'So dangerous. And because of the gay scene in New York, and the baths, unfortunately it was a perfect, terrible fit.'

In 1980, there were a few mystery cases; it's reckoned fifteen people had died that year of what would later be called AIDS. There were theories about what was happening, and how infections were spreading; but no one knew for sure. At the end of 1981, when the ABC network ran the first TV story on 'gay cancer', presenter Frank Gifford introduced the piece with: 'This is a terrible problem. How come nobody's paying any attention to it?'

The lack of acknowledgement that there was a social health crisis, and the silence surrounding AIDS, continued even as the epidemic spread. Given the unwillingness of the authorities to engage with the problem, self-organisation in the gay community became key. In 1982, the Gay Men's Health Crisis was founded, holding a fundraiser at Paradise Garage which raised $50,000. Attempts to meet with New York's mayor, Ed Koch, were blocked, however.

The information vacuum created panic and an increase in homophobia. Medical staff in local hospitals feared the disease could be airborne. Patients and their loved ones reported that staff members at St Vincent's refused any physical contact or even to enter the patients' rooms, leaving meals outside their doors.

Eventually, some explanations became apparent. A French researcher identified the retrovirus that causes AIDS: lymphadenopathy associated virus (LAV), which later became subsumed into the term 'human immunodeficiency virus' (HIV), and the notion of 'safe sex' – and condom use – began to be promulgated.

Keith, Kenny, and their downtown friends had been shaken by the death of performer and Club 57 and Mudd Club regular Klaus Nomi in August 1983. By the end of 1984, the signs that the crisis was escalating were clear: in New York City, the number of new cases were running at more than 2,000 a year.

The musician Arthur Russell was diagnosed at the end of 1986; he died six years later, aged 40. Arthur Russell's story in some ways mirrors Keith Haring's. He'd arrived in New York in 1973, and became a musical director of the Kitchen, and took inspiration from clubs of all sorts, and venues, and DJs (especially Nicky Siano). The influence of both the Kitchen and the Gallery can be heard in songs like 'Go Bang #5'.

Arthur had attended Keith's New Year's Eve party at the beginning of 1984. As Sasha Frere-Jones wrote in *The New Yorker* in 2004, 'Russell and Haring were both gay men who came to New York and got swept up in various artistic communities.'[32]

David Wojnarowicz was diagnosed in 1987 (he died in 1992). Photographer Robert Mapplethorpe was another victim; he died in 1989. Sasha Frere-Jones again: 'AIDS destroyed the foundations of downtown culture'.

Young men and women were having to deal with the early deaths of dear friends and colleagues, and the epidemic contributed to a loss of clubs and venues. Paradise Garage shut in September 1987, just a few weeks before the venue's founder/owner Michael Brody died from AIDS-related complications.

By this time, the St Mark's Baths in the East Village, where Keith met Juan, had been closed in a crackdown against places alleged to permit 'high risk' sexual activity linked to the spread of AIDS.

Death was also present in other guises in Keith's life. In August 1988, Jean-Michel Basquiat died of a heroin overdose (Keith was one of those asked to speak at the memorial service). Larry Levan was struggling with various drug issues – he'd

---

[32] *The New Yorker*, 8 March 2004.

become a little erratic, in life, and on the decks – and after the demise of Paradise Garage he failed to hold down a DJ residency at a short-lived Lower East Side club called Choice. It's said that he began to sell bits of his record collection for drug money.

Given the immediate and emergency situation, and the inextricable links between his art and life, it's not surprising that this darkness began to affect Keith's work. In the depiction of Juan's ejaculation, the sperm looks jaunty, magical. Six years later, 1988, Keith produced a set of ten drawings in which sperm is satanic, with curling black horns, carrying a deadly mutation.

One powerful work from 1985, *Michael Stewart – USA for Africa*, was Keith's response to the death of one of his young black artist friends. Stewart was arrested for allegedly drawing graffiti in the subway, and died in police custody. Jean-Michel Basquiat also produced a hard-hitting painting after the incident.

Keith's work depicts a naked black male being tortured by white hands as other characters sink beneath a flood of blood. A globe makes a link between brutality in the USA and apartheid in South Africa; the message has worldwide significance.

It's a work that can shock anyone who knows

Keith Haring only for being cute, funny, sexually explicit, and joyful. A lot of his earlier work, emerging from his commitment to progressive causes – his anti-Reagan cut-ups, for example – had a playful quality, but his work attacking racial inequality, including apartheid in South Africa, was usually far from cosy.

Similar tones become more frequent in later works created as the AIDS crisis deepened. The use of deep red blood is more frequent, his anger explicit. The radiant baby never went away, the dancing figures were never defeated, but unsurprisingly some of his output depicted sombre, even gruesome, images, and the urgency of the messages increased.

There are bystanders in the Michael Stewart piece holding their hands over their eyes, ears, or mouths. Such images – urging the viewer to look, hear, and speak out about injustice – began to feature many times in Keith's work relating to the AIDS crisis. The world needed to wake up. President Reagan's belated first public mention of AIDS came in 1985 when he said he wasn't sure whether children who were HIV+ should be allowed to attend school.

ACT UP, an organisation created to fight for visibility and an end to the AIDS crisis, emerged in March 1987 following a call to arms from Larry

Kramer, formerly a prime mover at the Gay Men's Health Crisis. ACT UP activists staged a series of direct actions, demonstrations and other interventions. Keith worked on a number of pieces which incorporated the powerful ACT UP slogans 'Silence = Death' and 'Ignorance = Fear', again featuring figures covering their eyes and ears and mouths.

Inevitably, given his nightlife connections, his AIDS activism also found an outlet after dark. For example, on 26 July 1989, Keith hosted a benefit for ACT UP at the Sound Factory, 530 West 27th Street (a former sewing factory). The party featured Junior Vasquez, one of Keith's favourite DJs; two years earlier, he'd invited him to DJ at the unveiling of a mural at an outdoor public swimming pool at Carmine Street and Seventh Avenue.

+

Keith Haring's life ended on 16 February 1990. *The New York Times* reported that at his memorial event, his art was hailed for 'its appeal to playful, childlike impulses as well as its conceptual sophistication and references to social issues', explaining that Keith 'embodied the young, exuberant art scene of lower Manhattan during the 1980's.'[33]

I asked Samantha if she'd ever imagined

during the early 1980s – as young energies spilled into and out of the venues and the streets of Lower Manhattan, careers being created, art and music suffusing, so much happening – that over three and a half decades later someone would be sitting with her in west London discussing her life back then, those energies, and those careers.

'No, not at all,' she replied. 'And that's because of what happened with AIDS. When AIDS took hold, people began to die literally in their hundreds. Juan died, and then Bobby Breslau died, and just after Keith died, John Sex died. And of course, Andy Warhol and Jean-Michel had died. The whole environment changed, people moved out, and people moved away.'

All the stories had come to an end?

'They'd come to an end, yes. It was gone. The world that had started in 1978 was gone, it was literally gone; artists, musicians, dancers, and the people writing about them.'

And yet, and yet…

Keith had faith in the future. On his deathbed, his final painful scribble was a radiant baby. He cherished the restlessness and resourcefulness of

[33] *The New York Times*, 5 May 1990.

youth: the virtues he never had the desire, or time, to grow out of.

He'd revelled in situations in which he could draw on the energies of the young. In 1987, he created a mural in Philadelphia called *We the Youth* depicting two or three dozen (almost life-size) dancing figures coloured blue, yellow, red, and green. It was made with the help of fourteen high-school students from New York and Philadelphia. His work, and life, was so much about collectivity; one section of the mural connected the two cities, containing the words 'We the Youth: City Kids of Phila + NYC'.

One of his final large-scale works, made in May 1989, was a mural on a huge piece of plywood. With De La Soul on the boom box, Keith worked alongside three hundred kids from local Chicago schools, encouraging them to add their own drawings, shapes, and slogans. One of the kids wrote in big letters, I WOULD FLY IF I HAD WINGS AND SOMEWHERE TO FLY.

During those days open-air in Chicago, Keith had the debut De La Soul album on the boom box; *3 Feet High and Rising* was entertaining and inspiring him and the kids. You can imagine even the artwork surrounding the band delighting him: colourful, cartoonish and full of positive 'daisy age' vibes.

ACT UP remained active, not just in America, but elsewhere. In Paris, the organisation lobbied the medical establishment with a series of disruptive interventions, and took strength from the nascent house music scene in the city. Their activities, including the links between AIDS activism and life after dark, are celebrated and documented in the 2017 film *BPM (Beats Per Minute)*.[34]

After 1990, the number of deaths from AIDS-related illnesses in New York continued to rise, peaked in 1994 (over 7,000 were reported that year), but are now in the low hundreds thanks to improved prevention education and screening techniques, and advances in medicine – including the evolution of antiretroviral therapy.

In 1989, and then 1990, a couple of club nights were created in London by Patrick Lilley and Norman Jay and others: 'High On Hope' and 'Queer Nation', both of them directly inspired by visits Norman and Patrick made to Paradise Garage in the mid-1980s.

In Manchester, as in many cities round the

---

[34] I have written about ACT UP Paris here: http://www.curzonblog.com/all-posts/dave-haslam-120bpm-dance-music-activism-actup-paris (consulted August 2019).

world, gay clubs until the late 1980s were mostly hidden away down unlit streets, or under railway arches on the edge of town, but things changed: the gay community became visible, and acknowledged. In 1990, on Canal Street in Manchester, Manto – the first of a new generation of gay bars – opened. It was sited directly on the street, glass-fronted, out and proud.

We've had several decades of progress, although it's probably the case that each generation has enjoyed provisional rather than permanent victories. Homophobia still has a vicious presence in the world. Nothing can be taken for granted; like a dance music addict, activism never sleeps.

By the second half of the 1980s, Samantha was out of New York; she'd moved on: 'The whole experience felt like a dream. I didn't think anyone would ever hear of it.'

Is it true that nothing lasts for ever – not youth, not life, and certainly not nightclubs? There we were in west London, Samantha and me talking of the collective energies unleashed in black-walled rooms down empty streets populated by art student beatniks and performance artists, and big dance-floors pulsing to uplifting disco music; and of individual talent, idealism and activism; of Kenny and

Keith, and Keith and Juan.

And as we talked, that same week, an exhibition of Nan Goldin photographs, including some with Mudd Club regulars, was showing at Tate Modern; the Guggenheim (New York) was featuring a Basquiat exhibition (the centrepiece, his Michael Stewart work); and Liverpool Tate was hosting the first major Keith Haring retrospective in the UK.

Two days before I visited Tate Liverpool – nearly thirty years after Keith's death – I was waiting at the tram stop at St Peter's Square in front of Manchester's Central Library, when I caught sight of my friend Vince. He introduced me to the young woman he was with, Nikki. She noticed I had Keith Haring's *Journals* in my hand. 'I love Keith Haring,' she told me, and showed me her ankle. A tattoo of a Haring dancing figure. And then she rolled up her sleeve and showed me a Keith Haring heart on her arm.

At the time of my tram stop encounter I was reading what Keith wrote in his *Journals* on his birthday in May 1982 during those averagely busy few months in the always hectic life of Keith Haring. On his way home from Rotterdam, while waiting for a plane at Brussels Airport, he was taking an hour to write down his thoughts.

His mood seems buoyant but also thoughtful. He's unsure how success will affect him but seems hopeful that his deeds and influence will last longer than he will. That perhaps it's possible to make an impact on the world that will maybe last for ever: 'I am making things in the world that won't go away when I do. If this "success" had not happened then maybe the world would not know these things after I go away. [...] These things that are called the works of Keith Haring.'

ORIGINAL ILLUSTRATION, DESIGN & TYPESETTING

Zoë McLean, Manchester
zoe@confingopublishing.uk

BODY TYPE

Minion 3, an updated and expanded version of Robert Slimbach's early 90s design for Adobe.

COVER TYPE

Futura PT, developed at ParaType in 1995 by Vladimir Yefimov, expands on the classic geometric sans-serif typeface Futura designed by Paul Renner in 1927.

ALSO IN THE ART DECADES SERIES

A Life in Thirty-Five Boxes:
How I Survived Selling My Record Collection

'Dave Haslam is a genius... Home truths, deep deep flavours. It's a joy'
Lemn Sissay MBE

'Cracking wee read'
Ian Rankin

'I found so much empathy and familiarity with what Dave so beautifully says that it was close to listening to an old friend'
Matt Bradshaw

'Looks and feels lovely – addresses so many issues and thoughts. It's almost in many ways not about the vinyl – it's brilliant on so many levels'
Dan Clapton

OTHER BOOKS BY CŌNFINGŌ PUBLISHING

Ornithology: Sixteen Short Stories Nicholas Royle

We Were Strangers: Stories Inspired by Unknown Pleasures (ed. Richard V. Hirst)

Pharricide Vincent de Swarte (translated by Nicholas Royle)

CŌNFINGŌ

confingopublishing.uk